BINDING THE
STRONG MAN

A part of the
"<u>Classics by the Archbishop</u>"
Series

ARCHBISHOP N. DUNCAN-WILLIAMS

Copyright © 2012 by Archbishop Nicholas Duncan-Williams

Binding the Strong Man
by Archbishop Nicholas Duncan-Williams

Printed in the United States of America

ISBN 9781600344084

All rights reserved solely by the author. The author guarantees all contents are original and do not infringe upon the legal rights of any other person or work. No part of this book may be reproduced in any form without the permission of the author. The views expressed in this book are not necessarily those of the publisher.

All Material is the property of Global Prayer Invasion©.
You may not reproduce or plagiarize this material
in any form, written or otherwise.

Unless otherwise indicated, Bible quotations are taken from the King James version of the Bible.

www.xulonpress.com

TABLE OF CONTENTS

Chapter 1	The Battle Line is Drawn	11
Chapter 2	Nature of the Conflict	13
Chapter 3	The Hierarchies	15
Chapter 4	Identifying the Strong Man	21
Chapter 5	Doorways of the Strong Man	29
Chapter 6	The Believer's Authority and Armor	43
Chapter 7	Keys to Binding the Strong Man	53

INTRODUCTION

The believer is God's law enforcement agent here on earth. According to the Scriptures, "The heaven, even the heavens, are the Lord's; but the earth has He given to the children of men" (Psalm 115:16).

God spoke to man and said, "Be fruitful and multiply; fill the earth and subdue; have dominion over the fish of the sea, over the birds of the air, and over every living thing that moves on earth" (Genesis 1:28).

The Scripture also says that God has crowned man with glory and honor and has put him in dominion over the works of His hands (Psalm 8:5). This is a position of supreme authority! The word *glory* is interpreted from a Hebrew word which means *weight*. This signifies that God has put some weight on man, and that means that He gave man authority and responsibility over the affairs of the earth. Man, therefore, became God's delegated authority and was to fully represent God's interest on the earth.

Satan, through his deceptive and manipulative acts, caused man to commit high treason. Satan stole the authority and dominion that God had given to man in the beginning.

Through the work of the cross, Satan has been defeated (Phil. 2:5-9). The authority Satan stole from Adam in the Garden of Eden has been recovered by Jesus Christ and has been handed over *to every believer in Christ from Pentecost to the rapture*. It must be noted that Satan's license of operation has not yet expired. It will expire after the rapture and his thousand-year reign on the earth subsequent to the rapture. After this time, he will then be cast into the bottomless pit (Rev. 20:1-3).

Satan is presently operating illegally here on the earth (1 Thess. 2:18; 2 Cor. 4:4; Eph. 2:2) and the believer must enforce the law and the will of God over him.

The present-day believer must study Scriptures, which are God's laws. We obtain understanding through the study of the Scriptures so that we gain the revelation of the mind of God and the intention of God about every aspect of life and creation. Principalities, powers, thrones, dominions, and authorities were created by the Word of God and are therefore subject to His words. (Col. 1:16).

Friend, it is only after we have gained understanding through study of God's Word that we can enforce the laws of God over all entities of darkness. We are required also to superimpose the written will of God over every situation of life. One of the main obstacles the enemy places in the path of believers is ignorance. Ignorance is very dangerous. In fact, your ignorance is the strength of the enemy!

The extent of information that you have about the strategies of the enemy will determine your level of advantage over him. National governments spend much of their resources to acquire information about their foes and even their friends (because a friend today could be a hidden enemy tomorrow). So much more so, we, as saints of God, would do well to acquire maximum knowledge about the covert operations of our enemy.

Satanic and demonic activities have intensified against the church in these end times because the enemy knows his time is short. I believe that by this book the Holy Spirit is empowering me to share with you the wealth of experiential knowledge that I have gained through many years in ministry.

Binding the Strong Man **was written to give you:**

1. Access to the strategies of Satan and his infernal host of wickedness.
2. insight on how to deal with the master spirits that exert their influence on specific locations, institutions, and even families.

3. Ways of identifying them spiritually.

I crave your indulgence to give this book your absolute concentration. Friend, please do not put this book down until you have read it all.

Because his book is based on experiential knowledge, and on research gained from battles fought over the years against the strong man and his host of agents, I believe strongly that this book will benefit you. Strange occurrences took place in the effort to write and publish this book. Files containing certain portions of this book repeatedly got lost. But, we have the victory through Jesus Christ!

It is my prayer that the Holy Ghost will keep you from every distraction and interference, and that God will give you absolute concentration.

This book is written to give believers the most valuable input each one needs to live a fruitful Christian life. Because of its depth of definition, it can also be used as a resource for teaching.

-Archbishop N. Duncan-Williams

Chapter One

THE BATTLE LINE IS DRAWN

"And I will put enmity between you and the woman, and your seed and her Seed; He shall bruise your head, and you shall bruise His heel" (Genesis 3:15).

The above verse of Scripture opens up the subject that is the basis of this book. In the continuing chapters, I will be taking you through the various aspects of this Scripture's impact.

The Bible makes it plain that a battle line has been drawn between two kingdoms, or two realms of authority. One is the kingdom of God, which is the kingdom of light and righteousness. The other is the kingdom of the devil, which is the kingdom of darkness and wickedness. The human race is the subject of this great conflict and is not exempt. Since the fall of man in the Garden of Eden, the battle has raged on, and each power has sought to possess control over the human race. This battle is more spiritual than physical. Its impact is felt in every activity of the human race and in the personal issues of our lives (Eph. 6:10-12).

Where Do You Stand?

In times of war, the safe place to be is to belong to one of the parties involved in the conflict; but the safest and most secure place is to belong to the winning side. "He who is not with Me is against Me and he who does not gather with Me scatters abroad" (Matt 12:30).

This scripture completely overrules any neutrality in the issue. My dear friend, if you do not now belong to the winning side in this war, I will ask you to turn to the last page of this book and confess out loud the prayer inscribed there. Mean it with your whole heart, *and the matter will be settled.*

In this conflict, the kingdom of God is the winning side. Jesus Christ is the King and Commander-in-Chief of God's army; every individual who has confessed and accepted Him as Lord and personal Savior is automatically recruited into His army.

Chapter Two

NATURE OF THE CONFLICT

A story is told of a man who was recruited to join the army during a tribal war in his village. The man was not trained to be a soldier but was simply recruited because of the war. Initially, he took everything casually; until after a few days of action, he realized that:

- *Bullets and arrows were flying past him.*
- *Bullets and arrows were being fired at him.*
- *They went out to recover the wounded and dead.*

It was only after some of these experiences that this newly recruited soldier realized and became fully aware that he was *at war*. This is the condition of many Christians today! They have not recognized the reality of the spiritual battle that is raging. Many people, including Christians, have a very casual attitude about this fierce, aggressive, and very dangerous spiritual conflict.

Spiritual battles are more aggressive and dangerous than physical ones. What is even more serious is that we are engaged in a conflict with an enemy who cannot be detected with the physical senses. Even so, he is real. The enemy is not imaginary, he is very real. Friend, you must become aware that:

- There is an enemy.
- The enemy is spiritual.

- The enemy operates from the spiritual realm.
- The first deception of the enemy is to make you believe that there is no enemy.
- The warfare we find ourselves involved in is dangerously aggressive.
- This warfare is with a very determined, very experienced, and well-organized enemy.
- You are one of the targets of this well-organized enemy.

But, friend, the *exciting* truth is that our Lord Jesus Christ, who is the King of kings and Lord of lords, overcame this enemy. He has given us the ability and the right to overcome the enemy, as well. *"Having wiped out the handwriting of requirements that was against us, which was contrary to us. And He has taken it out of the way, having nailed it to the cross. Having disarmed principalities and powers, He made a public spectacle of them, triumphing over them in it"* (Col. 2:14-15).

You are not fighting from the losing side of the battle, but from the exalted and victorious position of the battle. You and I have to enforce the written sentence and judgment over the enemy, and we will experience tremendous victories (Psalm 149:5-9).

Chapter Three

THE HIERARCHIES

Both the kingdom of God and that of Satan operate in hierarchical order. That is to say, there are grades of authority or status from the highest to the lowest ranks.

The Godhead also operates in the same order, and so do the angels of God who operate in various rankings with varying degrees of authority—chief or higher angels, lesser angels, in that order.

The hierarchy mentioned in Colossians 1:16-17— *"For by Him all things were created that are in heaven and that are on earth, visible and invisible, whether thrones or dominions or principalities or powers. All things were created through Him and for Him*—is different from the satanic hierarchy mentioned in Ephesians 6:12: *"For we do not wrestle against flesh and blood, but against principalities and powers, against the rulers of darkness of this age, against spiritual hosts of wickedness in the heavenly places."*

Take note that "rulers of darkness of this age" and "spiritual hosts of wickedness in heavenly places" are not mentioned in the Colossians account.

God has angelic thrones with accompanying delegated authority in various capacities, according to their assigned duties. Satan, who has nothing originating from him other than evil, has sought to duplicate the divine order with a rival setup to carry out his evil schemes.

An example is the story of Daniel, the Archangel Michael, and the Prince of Persia in Daniel 10:13: *"But the Prince of Persia withstood me for twenty-one days; and behold, Michael, one of the chief princes came to help me, for I had been left there alone with the kings of Persia"* and in Daniel 10:21, *"But I will tell what is noted in the Scripture of Truth: No one upholds me against these, except Michael, your prince."*

It is imperative for every believer to understand the principles that govern binding and loosing. In Matthew 16:19, Jesus says, *"And I will give you the keys to the kingdom of heaven, and whatever you bind on earth will be bound in heaven, and whatever you loose on earth will be loosed in heaven."* Whenever you bind or loose on earth, the angels of God are mandated to enforce your command in the heavens.

Psalm 103:20 says: *"Bless the Lord, you His angels who excel in strength, who do His word, heeding the voice of His word."* Do you realize that angels do God's word, and heed the voice of His word? *"The voice of His word"* refers to taking God's Word and vocalizing it. Remember, His Word is the two-edged sword that you hold in your hand as stated in Psalm 149:60: *"Let the high praises of God be in their mouth and a two-edge sword in their hand."* The Word of God is also sharper that any two-edged sword, it penetrates even to dividing soul and spirits, joints and marrow; it judges the thoughts and attitudes of the heart (Heb. 4:12).

The keys of the kingdom, related to binding and loosing, are the knowledge of all the devices of the devil. As surely as one cannot gain access to a room without a key, so also one cannot bind or loose without knowledge. Hosea 4:6 says: *"My people are destroyed for lack of knowledge. Because you have rejected knowledge, I also will reject you from being priests for Me."* Ignorance in any area of life is to the advantage of the enemy and to your disadvantage. He preys on you in any area of ignorance. Ignorance, therefore, is an unaffordable luxury.

The Infernal Kingdom

Ephesians 6:12 tells us: *"For we do not wrestle against flesh and blood, but against principalities, against powers, against the rulers of darkness of this age, against spiritual hosts of wickedness in heavenly places."*

The above Scripture gives us insight about the structures and setup of Satan's kingdom. I will take you through these, and we will carefully examine each one of them according to their order of rankings and their varying degrees of authority and spheres of influence.

Principalities

This word is translated from a Greek word *archias*. These are princes of the underworld who manipulate certain sections of the universe. Principalities are ruling spirits assigned over nations and cities.

Principalities are the highest of the rankings in the enemy's domain. They have been delegated the power to influence the affairs of nations and kingdoms and to resist God's purposes concerning these nations and kingdoms.

They exert their influence over heads of nations and kings; and they seek to control the political lives of these nations, using the human head as their main instrument of operation. They instigate kings and rulers to pass wicked and unrighteous laws. Most of these laws contravene the laws of Almighty God. The infamous Adolf Hitler, who committed untold atrocities on the Jewish people—exterminating six million of them in Nazi concentration camps—is an example of the work of principalities in modern history.

Principalities over the Russian nation gripped that nation and enslaved it for seventy years with Communism. The Russian nation extended its influence over almost half of the nations of the world and brought untold suffering to the citizenry of these nations.

In summary, the functions of principalities are:

- detailing and directing plans for countries and cities;
- Influencing men and women in government and positions of decision-making in nations (2 Tim. 2:2; Dan. 10:13)
- Directly carrying out the evil purposes of Satan.

The Powers

Powers is the second level of authority in Satan's kingdom. They exert their authority over the decision-making bodies of a nation, influencing the structures of all the governing authorities and promoting wickedness and injustice by controlling lawmakers, policy makers, and counselors in places of authority in the land.

One can read accounts of this in the Bible. For example, governors and counselors conspired against Daniel and convinced King Darius to issue decrees banning all religious activities in an attempt to get Daniel eliminated.

Daniel 6:3, 6-8 reads: *"Then this Daniel distinguished himself above the governors and satraps because an excellent spirit was in him; and the king gave thought to setting him over the whole realm ... So, these governors and satraps thronged before the king and said thus to him: King Darius, live forever! All the governors of the kingdom, the administrators and satraps, the counselors and advisers, have consulted together to establish a firm decree, that whoever petitions any god or man for thirty days except you, O King, shall be cast into the den of lions. Now, O King, establish the decree and sign the writing, so that it cannot be changed according to the law of the Medes and Persians, which does not alter."*

Note that Daniel, being the only righteous man in the government, was enough threat for the enemy to seek to destroy him by instigating the king to pass the decree.

Powers influence the thoughts and feelings of human beings. They can influence people to kill, steal, and indulge in all manner of destructive deeds. Friend, these powers can even influence Christians to gossip, to backbite, to slander people, to bear grudges against each other, even cause people to eat too much or cause them not to fast, or influence persons to decide not to participate in church activities.

They cause people to have a lackadaisical attitude to the work of God and convince them to want to spend more time watching television than reading their Bibles. These powers can draw Christians away from paying tithes—or should they intend to pay tithes, they are influenced not to pay the correct amount. The list can go on. These examples are cited to illustrate some of the influencing operations of the powers—even among believers.

This category of Satan's hierarchy also works hard to destroy peace and love between pastors, between pastors and congregation members, between Christians within the same church, between various churches or between denominations. They promote strife and contention amidst the Christian community.

They also exert influence in families to cause strife division. They are responsible for divorces and the breakdown of family unions.

They influence gangs and devilish fraternities and are responsible for the unruly behavior of certain individuals in educational institutions and within the society.

Powers make Christians believe a lie and get into a state of offense. They work through the media and promote Satan's agenda via the airwaves and the newspapers. Remember, one of Satan's titles is "the prince of the power of the air" (Eph. 2:2).

In summary, powers have the ability to:

- Influence the thoughts and feelings of human beings;
- Influence Christians for destructive purposes;
- Influence and operate through the media.

Rulers of Darkness

Next in the satanic hierarchy are the rulers of darkness of this age (Eph. 6:12). The word used in original Greek is *kosmokrateros*, which means *world rulers*. These powers are mandated by the devil to promote false religions and occult practices, thereby enslaving the souls of men in deception. It is not at all strange to see kings and rulers of nations striving to enforce false religions upon their people. In some nations, the penalty for being a Christian is death. Islam is one such ruler of darkness. Entire nations have the Koran as their constitution and the Sharia law is strictly enforced. It is the same in other nations with other false religions.

Friend, the main aim of these rulers of darkness is to control. They deceive human beings and place in their minds false teachings, false visions, and false dreams. They promote astrology, numerology, palmistry, fortune telling, divinations, horoscope, hypnotism, witchcraft, black and white magic, conjuration, charms, fetishes, and incantation. They also promote false religions such as Buddhism, Taoism, Hinduism, Islam, Shintoism, Confucianism, Eckankar, and the Baha'i faith.

Spiritual Host of Wickedness

After powers come spiritual hosts of wickedness in heavenly realms. They promote lawlessness and wickedness in the land, ensnaring souls of men into all manner of abominable sins—such as homosexuality, lesbianism, rape, all manner of lust and lasciviousness, suicides, and drug addiction, to mention but a few.

This category is sometimes difficult to identify. The key to their operations resides in the word *wickedness*. Witches and witchcraft operations are under this group. Also in this category are marine and water spirits—Satan's navy. The witches and territorial spirits are Satan's air force, and demons form his troops.

Spiritual wickedness is responsible for accidents, premature death, suicides, and the like. They delay the blessings of God's people through situations and circumstances that are orchestrated against them. They are responsible for unseen obstacles that retard the progress and advancement of God's people.

In summary:
- They are very injurious and destructive in nature.
- They may appear as angels of light; and by their deception they draw many souls into their nets of destruction.
- They sometimes try to influence and interfere with messages from the pulpit. They cause Christians to sleep during the preaching of the Word of God and are responsible for distracting their concentration at church services, depriving them of spiritual insight.
- They convince the unsaved that it is well with them.

Chapter Four

IDENTIFYING THE STRONG MAN

Who is the strong man? How does one identify the strong man? In this chapter, we shall find out.

The strong man is one who controls a stronghold—a place or territory under his influence. This territory is heavily fortified and impregnable.

It is important for us to see things the way they really are and not the way they appear to be. The Scripture says, *"Through faith, we understand that the worlds were formed by the word of God, so that things which are seen were not made of things which so appear"* (Heb. 11:3).

Friend, we can conclude from the above scripture that there is not only one world. The Scripture says *worlds*. There is a spiritual world and a physical world, and we need to understand that things that are seen are a manifestation of things that cannot be seen. If we are going to be able to identify the strong man, then we should be able to look at some things which are seen (physical things and conditions) and through these things *perceive* things which are not seen. The word *perceive* has to do with the operations of our spirit man—and this goes beyond the realm of the senses. You *perceive* by faith, and faith goes beyond the realm of the senses.

The Scripture says, *"Faith is the substance of things hoped for, the evidence if things not seen"* (Heb. 11:1). Friend, the only way to identify things which cannot be seen is by faith.

The apostle Paul, in 2 Corinthians 4:18 said, *"While we look not at the things which are seen: for the things which are seen are temporal, but the things which are not seen are eternal."*

There is a way to locate things that are not seen. It is through the laws of faith. Faith is absolute dependence and reliance on the Word of God.

Our Lord Jesus Christ, after rebuking Thomas for his attitude of unbelief, said to him, *"Thomas, because thou hast seen me, thou hast believed: blessed are they that have not seen and yet have believed"* (John 20:29). There is blessedness in believing without seeing.

The Strong Man

The strong man is a satanic personality in charge or responsible for a stronghold. The Scripture says, *"For the weapons of our warfare are not carnal, but mighty through God to the pulling down of strong holds"* (2 Cor. 10:4).

A strong man is a fortified entity that Satan builds to exalt himself against the knowledge and plans of God. Satan always tries to operate under the cover of darkness. The only thing that exposes him is the light of God's Word. The revelation and illumination that come through the Word of God are what expose Satan's strongholds.

It should be realized that as long as Satan's strongholds remain concealed, the strong man is safe—and he can operate without being identified. As soon as the strong man is identified, half of the victory is established. That is why identifying the strong man is of absolute importance.

A strong man may have other evil spirits operating under his domain or authority, but the strong man is the *ruling spirit*. Dealing with one of the sub-spirits (if I may call them such), does not solve the problem. The strong man must be bound.

For example, bitterness is a ruling spirit, and under its domain of authority are at least seven other spirits, namely:

Resentment	Hatred	Murder
Un-forgiveness	Temper	Violence
Anger		

Binding any of the sub-spirits does not solve the problem of bitterness in the life of a person bound by that spirit. Once the ruling spirit of bitterness has been identified and dealt with, the other sub-spirits can be expelled with ease.

Strongholds are personal or corporate. They are places or territories heavily fortified with satanic power and influence under the control of a strong man. They can either be geographical locations, areas of influence in institutions or organizations, areas of influence in families, or areas of influence in certain segments of the lives of individuals.

Strong Man over Bastions or Cities

Over every nation, Satan has a strong man who is his representative, who carries out all the satanic agendas for that nation. This strong man is in league with other satanic powers to enforce Satan's will and programs for that nation.

> And behold, a hand touched me, which set me upon my knees and upon the palms of my hands. And he said unto me, O Daniel, a man greatly beloved, understand the words that I speak unto thee, and stand upright: for unto thee am I now sent. And when he had spoken this word unto me, I stood trembling. Then he said to me, Fear not, Daniel: for from the first day thou didst set thine heart to understand, and to chasten thyself before thy God, thy words were heard, and I am come for thy words. But the prince of the kingdom of Persia withstood me one and twenty days: but lo, Michael, one of the chief princes, came to help me; and I remained there with the kings of Persia. Now I am come to make thee understand what shall befall thy people in the latter days: for yet the vision is for many days.
>
> Daniel 10:10-14

> Then there came again and touched me one like the appearance of a man, and he strengthened me. And he said, O man greatly beloved, Fear not: peace be unto thee, be strong, yea, be strong. And when he had spoken unto me, I was strengthened, and said, let my lord speak; for thou hast strengthened me. Then said he, Knowest thou wherefore I come unto thee? And now will I return to fight with the prince of Persia: and when I am gone forth, lo, the prince of Grecia shall come. But I will shew thee that which is noted in the Scripture of truth: and there is none that holdeth with me in these things, but Michael your prince.
>
> Daniel 10:18-21

Daniel, after receiving revelation and insight into God's prophetic agenda for the nation and people of Israel during the Babylonian captivity, set himself to seek the will of God.

As he fasted and prayed persistently over a period of three weeks on the earth, there was a great spiritual conflict going on in the heavens. The prince of the kingdom of Persia, Satan's strong man for the kingdom of Persia, tried to resist the heavenly angel from bringing the answer to Daniel's prayer. For twenty-one days a mighty battle was raging in the heavenly realm. Daniel's persistence in prayer activated the release of the archangel Michael who came to help the angel bear the answer to Daniel's prayer. It was only after this divine reinforcement and intervention that the angel bearing the response to Daniel's prayer broke through the resistance of the satanic strong man of the Persian kingdom.

Here we are given a vivid picture of the operations of strong men over nations. They resist the purposes of God for that nation and for His people in that nation, and they promote and enforce the purposes of Satan.

In this particular instance, it was only Daniel's persistence in prayer and continued fasting that activated the divine reinforcement to enable the messenger angel to break through the opposing realm of darkness. The messenger angel was confronted with opposition, not only from the prince of Persia, but from other ruling spirits in league with the prince of Persia. I also call these satanic rulers of the spirit world, territorial spirits.

Understanding is given us here as to why certain nations or geographical locations are gripped with certain vices that seem to defy every solution. Specific places are noted for vices such as violence, idolatry, prostitution, gambling, and homosexuality, to mention a few.

Some nations are open to the gospel, while other nations are not and remain securely closed to the gospel of our Lord Jesus Christ.

Let me share an interesting example. There is a town located between the borders of Brazil and Uruguay. The main street is the border that divides the two countries. One side of the street is Brazil and the other side is Uruguay. A missionary who tried sharing some gospel tracts found out to his amazement that on the Uruguayan side of the street, people were very unresponsive and hostile. But, when he crossed over to the Brazilian side of the street, people who had refused the tracts before now received them and even thanked him.

Needless to say, the missionary's curiosity was aroused. He tested the reactions of several more people and found out that the same pattern occurred each time. Later the missionary prayed about what had happened, and the words of our Lord Jesus Christ echoed in his mind and spirit: *"No one can enter a strong man's house and plunder his goods unless he first binds the strong man"* (Matt. 12:29).

What we discover from this account is glaringly clear: the strong man on the Brazilian side had been bound, while the strong man on the Uruguayan side had not—so his spoils of human souls could not be plundered.

Strong Man in Charge of Religions and Beliefs

The West African country of Benin is the stronghold of the voodoo religion. Slaves that were taken from Benin centuries ago brought this religion with them. Today a mixture of voodoo and Catholicism has become a dominant factor in nations of the Caribbean. In Haiti, voodoo has almost become the national religion.

In other nations, Catholicism is so entrenched that the people do not want to know anything about the gospel of our Lord Jesus Christ and its power to heal and deliver.

In other societies, strongholds of witchcraft, Satanism, New Age religions, occultism, animism, and traditional worship have so completely bound the minds and hearts of people that they practice things to their own hurt. Because of some of these beliefs, ritual murders are committed and people indulge in human sacrifices for protection and for the acquisition of money and power. Many terrible and abominable things occur under the influence of such a strong man.

Strong Man in Charge of Families

Certain trends, that can be traced in a particular family for generations, where a vicious cycle of misfortunes is repeated, show the influence and control of a strong man.

In some families, anyone who tries to excel in life dies young. The strong man who rules over that family has set limitations in that family. Those who try to go beyond the limitations face a penalty of death.

➤ In other families divorce is inevitable. There can hardly ever be stable marriages in such families.

➤ In some families drunkenness has a consistent history. Men born into such families spend all their money on alcohol, leaving nothing to meet the needs of the home.

In other cases, the issue is a malignant disease that seems to be hereditary from one generation to another. People born into such families seemingly inherit the diseases.

Any negative and common trend that runs through a family from generation to generation is an indication of the operations of a strong man.

Strong Man Responsible for Individuals

Satan builds up personal strongholds to influence the lives of particular individuals. In some lives, it becomes evident that the individuals cannot overcome certain sins, certain ways of thinking, certain ways of feeling, certain attitudes or behavior patterns (even when the individuals know these things are not right).

Friend, every uncontrollable and consistent negative attitude or emotional reaction is controlled by a strong man. For some people, it is pride. For others, it is selfishness. For others, it can be wrath or anger—or what people call having a bad temper. Here, people acknowledge they have a bad temper and acknowledge that it is not good, yet they cannot do anything about it.

Bad habits which have persisted for years, which hold men and women in captivity, are controlled by a strong man.

There are many other operations of different strong men which must be identified and the strong men bound for the release of their captives. In identifying the strong man that rules in a place, the following must be carefully investigated:

- the prevalent lifestyle of the people;
- the culture and traditions that dominate that geographic area;
- the extent of the penetration of the gospel and persistent challenges.

Chapter Five

DOORWAYS OF THE STRONG MAN

How does the strong man gain access to establish a stronghold? How does the strong man entrench himself? What are some of the ways of ejecting that strong man? In this chapter we shall look into these considerations and further operations of the strong man.

"When a strong man, fully armed, guards his own palace, his goods are in peace. But when a stronger than he comes upon him and overcomes him, he takes from him all his armor in which he trusted, and divides his spoils" (Luke 11:21-22).

Please note that there are five main themes from the scripture above.

1. The strong man is fully armed.
2. He has his own palace.
3. He has goods or spoils.
4. He trusts in his armor.
5. There is one stronger than him.

First of all, the strong man is fully armed. He has fortifications and possesses weapons—both in demons under his command carrying out his wishes and in points of contact that give him the legal basis of carrying out his operations.

Secondly, the strong man has his area of jurisdiction of operations (the Bible refers to his palace). He has a central point from where his strategies are mapped out and from where his operations are monitored.

Thirdly, the strong man claims ownership over whatever falls under his area of influence. His goods and spoils can be either human souls, that he has enslaved, or they can be families where no one can excel.

Fourthly, the strong man's source of confidence is his armor.

Lastly—and most importantly—there is one stronger than him. In other words, the strong man is not invincible, only a localized champion.

In 1 Samuel 17:4, Goliath is referred to as the champion from Gath. Note that Goliath's reputation as a champion was limited to only Gath. Goliath assumed that he could also become a champion over Israel as he was in Gath in the land of the Philistines.

Before we go further, let me emphasize that Satan and his kingdom are outlaws. They will always try to exert their influence over areas outside their territories. And, they will do it when they are not resisted by the Word of God. First Peter 5:8 warns: *"Be sober, be vigilant; because your adversary the devil walks about like a roaring lion, seeking whom he may devour. Resist him, steadfast in the faith."*

When David came on the scene, he reminded Goliath that he was a champion in Gath and not in Israel and that in Israel there was somebody who was stronger than him—Jehovah the Lord God of Israel!

How Does the Strong Man Gain Access?

The strong man is a spirit being, a personality without a physical body. I believe that in accordance with the laws that Almighty God has set to govern the entire universe and especially the planet earth, no living soul can function without flesh and blood. A strong man therefore needs the body of a human being or an animal—most preferably a human being—to successfully complete its operations (Matt. 12:43-45).

For a strong man to gain access into any human life, he needs a doorway.

Access through the Occult and Idolatry

Idolatry and occultism come from the same root. Idolatry is the worship of demons. Occultism is the manipulation of demon powers for selfish goals (Psalm 106:35-42; 1 Cor. 10:20). The Word of God declares, *"Thou shalt not make thee any graven image, or any likeness of any thing that is in heaven above, or that is in the earth beneath, or that is in the waters beneath the earth: Thou shalt not bow down thyself unto them, nor serve them: for I the Lord thy God am a jealous God, visiting the iniquity of the fathers upon the children to the third and fourth generation of them that hate me. And shewing mercy unto thousands of them that love me and keep my commandments"* (Deut. 5:7-10).

God, in His Word, has given very clear instructions about idolatry and the consequences for it. When people disobey God because of their cultural or traditional practices (Mark 7:13) or they get involved in idolatry or occultism, they establish *covenants* with strong men (who are spirit personalities).

A *covenant* is a formal agreement made between two or more parties, which is binding on all the parties involved. Most of the time, these covenants are sealed with blood. It is either the blood of the individual involved or the blood of animals. This produces a blood covenant, which is the strongest covenant on the earth.

In these covenants, an agreement is made between a person or group of persons on one side and a deity on the other side. These covenants can be made for the purposes of protection, long life, success, prosperity, childbirth, and the like. The deity promises to bless the individuals involved in the agreement, and the individuals promise to worship the deity.

Once this agreement, which is legal and binding on all the parties, is established, the deity—or strong man—has a doorway into the life of that person or group of persons. *Unfortunately, the strong man does not only have access to that individual; but he also has access into the lives of generations yet unborn,* according to Deuteronomy 5:9 and Exodus 20:3-6.

The blessings promised by the strong man become a curse to the benefactor. The spiritual gifts, as well as the curse, are passed down from one generation to another. The root of idolatry and the occult is a major doorway through which the devil and his demons gain ways to operate.

Access through Sin
Sin in any shape, form, or kind is another major doorway for a strong man to entrench and fortify himself into the life of an individual.

"Soulish" Domination or Manipulation
If a parent is domineering and over-protective of a child, always wanting the child to do his and her will even when it is against the will of the child, it can be very dangerous. Rejection or rebellion can be produced. Rejection and rebellion are doorways for a strong man to enter.

Soulish domination, manipulations, and controlling powers can also be applied to husband-wife relationships. There can be soulish domination and manipulation of a pastor toward his congregation members. It can be seen in master-servant relationships, as well. Manipulation and domination are further doorways for a strong man to slip in.

Access through Circumstances and Situations
Life circumstances or situations can be doorways for the strong man to gain access into the lives of individuals. In moments of weakness, whether it is physical, spiritual, emotional, or financial, people unconsciously lose their ability to resist evil powers. That is when strong men move in quietly to establish strongholds.

For example, in moments of sickness, an individual can be depressed, afraid, anxious, and deeply troubled. This may not only affect the individual but a whole family. In such a state, resistance against evil is very low and the strong man moves in. In times of anger, bitterness, jealousy, or resentment, the strong man moves in and takes advantage of the situation to carry out the will of the devil.

Access through the Mass Media
Communication is another doorway through which a strong man can have access into the lives of people. Films, books, newspapers,

magazines, radio, television, and all media are quick doorways for a strong man to have access into the lives of people. When people watch a pornographic film or read a pornographic book or magazine, a strong man of fornication and adultery can be transferred. When people watch films whose contents are very violent, there is a negative impact on them.

Curses and the Strong Man

Another area that can give the strong man access to your life is through curses. A curse offers the strong man a legal ground to operate in one's life. The frustrating thing about this scenario is that one can be a born-again Christian and filled with the Holy Spirit and yet be living under a curse.

The fact that something is legally yours does not matter to the enemy. Satan and his cohorts are determined to deprive you of what is legally yours because he is an outlaw and does not leave you alone based solely on the fact that you are redeemed from his control.

The same is true concerning sickness and diseases. Even though God's Word teaches that we were healed by the stripes of Jesus almost two thousand years ago, it is our duty to appropriate the Word in order for it to work on our behalf. Otherwise, we will not enjoy the blessing of divine healing. Therefore, be aware that a believer is not legally under a curse but can be under the *influence* of a curse.

Every promise of God must be appropriated and fought for. A curse, according to biblical definition, is God's recompense in the life of man and his descendants as a result of iniquity.

Words are spirits. Whenever a word is spoken, the spirit of that word is released to ensure the fulfillment of that word. When a word of blessing is spoken, the spirit of that word will ensure that the word comes to pass—irrespective of the time duration. Therefore, blessings can be inherited from past generations.

In the same sense, when an evil word or a curse is uttered, the spirit behind that word will carry out the contents of that evil word or curse.

One can be cursed right from the womb and one can also be blessed from the womb. *"You show loving kindness to thousands, and repay the iniquity of the father in the bosom of their children after them"* (Jer. 32:18).

Some individuals, because of a curse, are estranged from the womb (Psalm 58:3). Children can be born with curses. Curses also give the strong man control over households. The strong man cannot be bound unless the curses that give him legal grounds are broken.

Breaking the Curse

"Christ has redeemed us from the curse of the law, having become a curse for us (for it is written, *'Cursed is everyone who hangs on a tree')"* (Gal. 3:13; Deut. 27:26).

You can break every curse in your life by standing on this verse. After breaking the curse, the strong man lacks any ground to operate.

Prayer for Breaking the Curse

Heavenly Father, in the name of Jesus, I repent and renounce every sin in my life. I renounce every spell, hex, and demonic invocation and revoke every satanic prophecy that is operating in my life. I also reverse every divination and enhancement working in my life, family, business, and all that concerns me. In the name of Jesus, I bind the strong man and all his agents; and I break every curse enforced against me.

I break curses of destruction, sickness, and premature death. I break curses of poverty, lack, debt, and insufficiency. In the name of Jesus, I exercise dominion and authority over the strong man operating under any curse in my life; and I release my inheritance from the strong man. I declare that I am redeemed from the curse of the law by the blood of Jesus, and I loose myself and those of my household from all curses and their effects in the name of Jesus Christ the Son of the living God.

I command the strong man and all his demons to leave me in Jesus' name. Amen.

Operation of the Strong Man

As I have already pointed out, the strong man does not operate in isolation, but has a host of other spirits operating under him. In other words, the strong man has a stronghold made up of demons that execute his orders.

The strategies employed by the strong man have one ultimate goal—to stop people, societies, and nations from fulfilling their dreams and God's plan for their lives. It is his aim to abort the purposes of God. When God created man, His aim for man was for fellowship between man and Himself. This was cut off in the Garden of Eden. However, God, in His abundant mercies, through Jesus Christ, has restored this fellowship.

Through the ages, Satan sought to make the coming of Jesus impossible so that this fellowship would not be restored. He schemed and employed human beings, institutions, and establishments— knowingly or unknowingly—to pervert the course of justice and impose legislations contrary to the Word of God.

In chapter three of this book, I explained the hierarchies and chain of command within the satanic kingdom. In that chapter, we examined some of the Satan's operations through his command structure. Let us examine briefly, more examples from the Word of God. We shall look at the accounts of Moses, Esther, Jesus, Joseph, and David to see how Satan employs legal and political systems against the people of God.

Moses

Before the birth of Moses, the people of Israel, then in Egypt because of Joseph, grew in all areas of their lives. A new king arose in Egypt who, according to the Scriptures, "knew not Joseph" (Exodus 1:8). Satan used this new king, a strong man, to oppress the Israelites. Satan, knowing that the deliverer of God's people was soon to appear, caused the new king to issue a decree to kill all newly born males among the Israelites (Exodus 1:16), and his aim was to abort the plan of God for the people of Israel, for them to remain in bondage; and he used legislation.

Today, Satan is still in the same business. That is why legislations in many countries do not conform to the Word of God.

When Satan's first plans failed, he caused the strong man of Egypt to issue another decree for all males born to Israelites to be thrown into the river Nile (Exodus 1:22). It would be easy to deduce that the sons of Israel were to be used as sacrificial offerings to the gods of Egypt. All this happened to kill the deliverer of the nation of Israel. Please be aware that the enemy is fighting you, tooth and nail, to keep you from succeeding in life.

Satan is not omnipresent, and neither is he omnipotent. Otherwise, he would have pinpointed the specific family from which Moses was to be born, but he isn't which is why he needs a network of agents to carry out his commands.

Jesus *is* all-knowing. If we have Jesus living inside of us, then greater is He who lives in us than he who is in the world (1 John 4:4). By the help of the Holy Spirit, God has also made available to us revelation gifts—the gift of the word of knowledge and the gift of discerning spirits, among them—with which we are able to detect the operations of the enemy. Friend, these gifts have been given to profit us. Let us desire them and walk in them. The apostle Paul said, *"We are not ignorant of his* [the devil's] *devices"* (2 Cor. 2:11).

Esther

The main focus of this account is how Satan sought, through legislation, to exterminate the Jews. He employed the services of Haman, a strong man in the flesh. However, Mordecai got wind of the plan and helped Queen Esther to avert Satan's purpose (Esther 3 through 5:14).

One operation of Satan is to place his own people in strategic position in a society so that they will carry out his agenda. It is our duty as Christians to remove men and women who the enemy has planted in the corridors of power from their office, through prayer.

Jesus

When Jesus was born, the enemy orchestrated a plan to get rid of Him, knowing that Christ was to save mankind. Satan worked through Herod who was a schemer and a wicked ruler.

This is Herod's background: He was the son of Antipar, who wormed his way into the confidence of Julius Caesar. The Romans made him procurator of Judea. Later the descendant of the Maccabean dynasty, Antigonus, was executed. Herod craftily managed to stay in power despite the changing government of Rome. He was so evil that Caesar Augustus is credited with saying that, "I would rather be Herod's dog than his son."

Satan made full use of Herod to slaughter innocent infants in Bethlehem in an attempt to kill the Messiah. But God averted this by revealing to Joseph the enemy's plans. Joseph was sent to Egypt for the safekeeping of Jesus. *As long as we stay in God's camp, He will reveal the strategies of our enemy.*

Joseph and David

The strong man sometimes operates through frame ups. Take Joseph's case as an example. The enemy employed Potiphar's wife to try to seduce Joseph into committing adultery. Joseph spurned her and fled, leaving his jacket behind. Because she failed to get him to do what she wanted, she chose to frame Joseph, using his jacket to accuse him of rape. Who would not believe her? She was the wife of Potiphar, a respected member of the personal staff of Pharaoh, the king of Egypt. If Joseph had indeed committed this sin, who knows what would have become of his dreams? Child of God, be wary, for Satan is the accuser of the brethren.

Spirit beings without human bodies are able to influence humans who do not understand, to use the media—both electronic and print—to halt the purposes of God for individuals and for nations. Satan works against God's agents of change right in their corridors of power. He does it by discrediting them and thereby rendering them ineffective in bringing in the necessary change.

Satan uses people with all sorts of false allegations and half-truths to knowingly or unknowingly discredit individuals, organizations, churches, and men of God. His plan is to get the world to not hear them even when they have a message of truth. Within these wrong perceptions, people turn to and prefer other leaders. This can cause vexation—leading a person into jealousy and anger, even to provoking such a person to self-destruction.

David committed sin by taking a census after he was provoked by the devil. Second Chronicles 21:1 says, "And Satan stood up against Israel and provoked David to number Israel."

Satan, the adversary, is mentioned in the Bible by the use of more than thirty different names and titles. Each one speaks about some aspect of him or his work. Among the many names are:
- serpent (Gen. 3:4)
- king of devils (Matt. 12:24)
- prince of this world (John 14:30)
- god of this world (2 Cor. 4:4)
- tempter (1 Thess. 3:5)
- prince of the power of the air (Eph. 2:2)

Let us examine names of the strong man through the Scriptures.

Behemoth

This spirit is a strong man who controls some of the systems and religions that oppress multitudes of people. The control can be over political or religious systems. Behemoths must be bound and their strongholds plundered to release people to come to Christ. Persistent prayer and corporate fasting can break Behemoth's powers. The Scripture cited at the end of this paragraph discloses the strength of this spirit, *which must not be underestimated* (Job 40:15-24).

Leviathan

Following the above account in Scripture, we are told of another strong man who appears invincible (Job 41:1-34). Leviathan is represented in Scripture as a crocodile, a crooked serpent, and a dragon.

Leviathan promotes wickedness in various forms. This spirit also hardens the hearts of men against God and causes them to walk in pride. Pride is to seek to be independent of God and to walk in self-deception, or to have an exaggerated impression of oneself. People under the influence of this strong man are very resistant to the gospel. They will maintain a religious gap and be sources of rebellion against spiritual authority.

Reading the whole of Job 41, one discovers the incredible adamancy and strongholds of these spirit beings, Behemoth and Leviathan. The answer to paralyzing the strong man lies in the book of the prophet Isaiah 27:1: *"In that day the Lord with His severe sword, great and strong, will punish Leviathan the fleeing serpent,*

Leviathan the twisted serpent; and He will slay the reptile that is in the sea."

"In that day" in the above Scripture refers to *"the day of awakening,"* when the children of God will rise up to exercise their divine rights by binding up those spirits. Please note that the only weapon used in this combat will the sword of the Lord—the Word of God.

Belial

Belial is the ruling spiritual wickedness, and has a host of wicked spirits that operate under his authority. The name Belial comes from a Hebrew word, *Beliiyual*, which means without profit, worthlessness, destruction, wickedness, and mighty evil stubbornness. The work of this spirit is to cause men to commit contemptible and vile sins—sins that are so vile as to rouse moral indignation.

All sin is sin, but some sins are more abominable than others. When Belial is in control of a family, rape, incest, and sodomy can be found running in the family. These sins seem to have an unbreakable control over that family.

In 2 Samuel 23:6-7, the Bible compares the sons of Belial to thorns that cannot be handled or taken with the hands: *"But the sons of Belial shall be all of them as thorns thrust away, because they cannot be taken with hands: But the man that shall touch them must be fenced with iron and the staff of a spear; and they shall be utterly burnt with fire in the same place."*

The latter part of this Scripture says that they who can conquer these spirits "must be fenced with iron." The iron here refers to the whole armor of God. It is completely impossible to deal with this spirit with human strength. Beloved, is any member of your family under the influence of such a strong man? Jail will not solve the problem. Medicine will be of little help in surpassing the outward symptoms. Total freedom of this spiritual strong man comes only by putting on the whole armor of God, taking the Word of God—the sword of the Spirit, and enforcing it.

Jezebel

Jezebel is the strong man of idolatry, seduction, rebellion, and sexual sins. He/she is also the spirit that opposes spiritual authority in the church by inciting the people to spiritual harlotry.

This strong man loves to masquerade as a prophet of God to undermine the true prophets of God. When not identified, this spirit can bring much havoc into the church.

Jezebel is also the strong man of witchcraft—both in the church and in domineering, abusive, manipulative, and exploitative persons. Such individuals will always seek to enforce their will and will not be subject to authority in a godly setup. Jezebel is a spirit who manifests his/her operations in both men and women.

In Revelation 2:20-22, Jesus rebukes the church for allowing Jezebel to have her way and threatens to destroy her and her followers.

The spirit of Jezebel must be confronted and dealt with *without any compromise*. Again in this case, *it is the Word of God that is the sole weapon* to defeat, bind, and paralyze this spirit.

Other Doorways That Give Access to the Strong Man

Uncleanness	Seared conscience
Immorality	Demonic doctrines
Sodomy	Debauchery
Whoredom	Delusion
Witchcraft	Sorcery
Deception	Flightiness
Uncontrolled lust	Sexual impurities
Infirmities	Idolatry
Adultery	Shamelessness
Obscenity	Apostasy
Blasphemy	Rebellion
Poverty	Lesbianism
Drug addiction	Homosexuality

There certainly could be more than these could listed here, but whenever you notice that any one of the above is in control of an individual, family, church community, or nation, you can be sure that a strong man is in operation.

Modus Operandi

God, by His grace and mercies, through the shed blood of our Lord Jesus, has given the believer authority over the strong man.

Much of how to bind the strong man has been covered in the previous pages of this book, but I would like to emphasize the following points. If one wants to overcome the strong man, one must close all the doorways and deny him access to one's life.

- *You must be born again.* That means you must renounce sin in your life and receive Jesus Christ as your Lord and personal Savior. Believe and confess Him as your Lord (Romans 10:9-10).
- By prayer, claim the whole armor of God as your spiritual clothing.
- Claim victory by the blood of Jesus over the strong man, and call upon the hosts of God to come against him.
- Use the Word of God, which is the sword of the Spirit, against him.
- Aggressively command the strong man to be bound in Jesus' name, and command that which was bound to be loosed.

Chapter Six

THE BELIEVER'S AUTHORITY AND ARMOR

The word *authority* is translated from a Greek word which means the right to use power. It also means the right to have one's words and commands obeyed.

The policeman is empowered by the government to enforce the law and to deal with lawbreakers. He has the power to arrest and detain those who disobey the law. When a judge declares someone guilty and passes out a sentence, it is the duty of the law enforcement and penal agent to see to it that this sentence is executed.

This is exactly how the believer stands in Christ. We are mandated to enforce the laws of our God over the spiritual lawbreakers, who sometimes carry out their activities through human agents. Friend, you need to realize that even though a policeman may be physically feeble, his ability is not undermined, even to stop a trailer on the road. He has something more powerful than the power of the trailer's engine or tires. He has *authority*. He only has to lift his hand to signal stop, and the trailer comes to a halt.

The believer has the *power of attorney* to use the name of Jesus to bring the devices of the enemy to a halt. This illustration about the policeman is used to simplify understanding that the extent to which you utilize your God-given authority will determine how far the enemy advances with his evil intentions.

The Scripture says, *"Behold I give you authority to tread on serpents and scorpions and over all the power of the enemy: and nothing shall by any means hurt you"* (Luke 10:19).

Friend, you and I have been authorized by heaven as God's ambassadors to carry out and enforce the laws of Jehovah. We have the backing of the powers of heaven in this assignment. Just as the policeman is fully backed by the government of his nation, the believer has heavenly backing. The Scriptures say, *"Let the saints be joyful in glory: let them sing aloud on their beds. Let the high praises of God be in their mouth, and a two-edged sword in their hands, to execute vengeance on the heathen, and punishments on the people; to bind their kings with chains, and their nobles with fetters of iron; to execute upon them the written judgment. This honor have all His saints"* (Psalm 149:5-9).

Just as it is dangerous to defy the laws of the state, so is it dangerous for the enemy to defy the commands of the believer. Whenever the policeman takes off his uniform and cap, which are symbols of his authority and by which he is recognized and respected, he loses the authority. The believers who rebel against the laws of the kingdom of God lose their right and mandate to exercise authority over the devil (2 Cor. 10:3-6).

Improper Dressing

God has provided a type of uniform for His saints to put on, and you must make sure you have yours on. You must be properly dressed.

The Christian life is a life full of battles. We have to be prepared as soldiers of the Lord at all times to wage spiritual warfare. The only way we can successfully do this is to put on the whole armor of God. We cannot let down our guard.

Can you imagine a soldier without his boots or helmet in battle? How about a soldier without his belt or a soldier dressed without his sword or gun? Yet most believers are not properly dressed spiritually, and many choose to select the pieces of armor that appeal to them and ignore the rest. This makes them vulnerable to the attacks of the enemy because the enemy takes advantage of the uncovered or unprotected areas.

The tendency for many Christians to dwell on just one part of the armor, such as faith, is dangerous. Each piece of the armor has its specific role, and one cannot be substituted for the other. Child of God, always remember that the armor is of God, and not of man (Eph. 6:10-19).

Before I proceed, I want to stress and remind you that in dealing with the strong man, you are not dealing with only one entity, but rather with a host of demons which are under the command of the chief entity—Satan. Therefore, victory over the strong man means overrunning the strongholds as well. In view of this, one must be *totally* equipped to be successful.

The Whole Armor of God

> Finally, my brethren, be strong in the Lord and in the power of His might. Put on the whole armor of God that you may be able to stand against the wiles of the devil. For we do not wrestle against flesh and blood, but against principalities, against powers, against the rulers of the darkness of this age, against spiritual wickedness in the heavenly places. Therefore take up the whole armor of God that you may be able to withstand in the evil day, and having done all, to stand. Stand therefore, having girded your waist with truth, having shod your feet with the preparation of the Gospel of peace; above all, taking the shield of faith with which you will be able to quench the fiery darts of the wicked one. And take the helmet of salvation, and the sword of the Spirit, which is the word of God.
>
> Ephesians 6:10-17

God has not left us at the mercy of the enemy but has equipped us with weapons to walk in total victory every day in our Christian lives. The above Scripture opens God's armory to us. In the "binding of the strong man," every believer will do well to make use of these weapons. Note there are two categories—the defensive and the offensive weapons. We shall examine each piece of the armor.

Always remember that *"though we walk in the flesh, we do not war after the flesh: For the weapons of our warfare are not carnal, but mighty through God to the pulling down of strongholds; casting down imaginations, and every high thing that exalteth itself against the knowledge of God, and bringing into captivity every thought to the obedience of Christ; and having in a readiness to revenge all disobedience, when your obedience is fulfilled"* (2 Cor. 10:3-6).

Weapons of Defense

Belt of Truth

Our first weapon of defense is truth. To walk in truth is to oppose all manner of falsehood. To walk in truth is to walk in fidelity to the Word of God. To put on the belt of truth is to walk in integrity of heart, sincerity, transparency, and openness, to God, to you, and to others. It means the absence of pretence, insincerity, and hypocrisy.

To explain the uses of the belt of truth, we must examine the physical uses of a natural belt. The belt goes around the middle part of our bodies to ensure that our clothes stay on.

"The wicked flee when no one pursues. But the righteous are bold as a lion" (Prov. 28:1). Walking in truth is the basis of our boldness. Absence of boldness is fearfulness. A fearful man is a loser before he starts anything.

This explains why Gideon was asked to send back home all those who were of a fearful heart. *"Now therefore, proclaim in the ears of the people, saying, 'Whosoever is fearful and afraid, let him turn and depart at once from Mount Gilead.' So twenty-two thousand men left, while ten thousand remained"* (Judg. 7:3).

Moses, the man of God, was also instructed to give similar warnings to the Israelites whenever they were ready for war. *"The officers shall say speak further to the people and say, 'What man is there who is fearful and faint-hearted? Let him go and return to his house, lest the heart of his brethren faint like his heart'"* (Deut. 20:8).

Another reason why the belt of truth must be in place is because the Bible says that Satan, the accuser of the brethren, accuses us day and night before our God (Rev. 12:10). On the other hand, we overcome Satan by the blood of the Lamb and the word of our testimony (Rev. 12:11). Two things are required that we *must employ* to defeat the accusations of Satan—the blood of Jesus and the word of our testimony.

Below is a prayer that you can pray to ensure that your belt of truth is in place.

Father, in the name of Jesus, I come before You on the basis of the shed blood of Jesus, and I invoke the speaking of the blood of Jesus against every accusation the enemy has brought against me. And I declare that every accusation of the enemy against me is overruled and canceled by the blood of Christ Jesus. I renounce every falsehood in my life in the name of Jesus Christ. Amen.

Breastplate of Righteousness

"And he [Abraham] *believed in the LORD, and He accounted it to him for righteousness"* (Gen. 15:6). Righteousness means to have a right standing with God. It has to do with our relationship with God. Righteousness cannot be earned by our work. Righteousness is higher than good works. It is imputed unto us as Christians when we become born again. That means, that to put on the breastplate of righteousness, I have to make sure that I walk in the righteousness of God and not in my own righteousness. Isaiah explains this better: *"But we are all like an unclean thing. And all our righteousnesses are like filthy rags"* (Isa. 64:6).

Even though the Lord has clothed us with His righteousness, it is our responsibility to keep it on by living lives compatible to His Word. It means to walk a walk of cleanliness and to guard our hands against any corruption.

"Keep your heart with diligence for out of it springs the issues of life" (Prov. 4:23). The breastplate covers the chest. Underneath the chest is one of man's most vital organs, the heart. Our hearts influence our affections, and our affections influence everything else in our lives. It is amazing when you begin to ponder why God placed the heart of man in his chest. Man's heart is protected by ribs, and when we put on the breastplate of righteousness, we protect our heart and all that has to do with it.

Feet Shod with the Preparation of the Gospel of Peace

A soldier must always be prepared for battle. He has to be instant *in season* and *out of season*. You cannot bind the strong man and overrun his stronghold when you are not prepared for battle.

To shod your feet with the gospel of peace is to wear shoes that are able to speed you on as you preach the Good News. It means we have to be ready and eager to preach or share the gospel always. It means we have to put on our boots for battle.

Boots are put on by the soldier for two reasons. Firstly, they help the soldier to stand firm. They keep him from slipping and sliding on difficult terrain. Sharing the gospel solidifies and stabilizes you in faith. The responsibility falls on us believers to study to know the Word of God, so that we can share it in confidence to have stability at all times. The second reason for putting on boots is that boots increase one's mobility. They enable one to move quickly and fearlessly over rough or unfamiliar ground.

"How beautiful upon the mountains are the feet of him who brings good news, who proclaims peace, who brings good tidings, who proclaims salvation, who says to Zion, 'Your God reigns'" (Isa. 52:7).

The weapons of our warfare must be used in unison. For example, prayer alone cannot save your family members from the control of the enemy. Prayer has to be used with of the Word of God. The Word of God, which is the gospel of peace, must be used alongside prayer.

The Shield of Faith

"Above all, taking the shield of faith with which you will be able to quench the fiery darts of the wicked one" (Eph. 6:16).

There are many definitions of faith, but the faith that is spoken of in the above scripture refers to unreserved confidence in God, absolute dependence on the integrity of God's Word, and complete reliance on the goodness of God. Faith is an unquestioning belief in God. *"But without faith it is impossible to please Him, for he who comes to God must believe that He is, and that He is a rewarder of those who diligently seek Him"* (Heb. 11:6).

The shield of faith, the Scripture says, will enable you to "quench the fiery darts of the wicked one." Those fiery darts are flame-tipped arrows, and there is usually a barrage of them that is released before a main assault. They are sent out by Satan to weaken your resolve and faith in God so that he can overpower you.

Fiery darts represent fierce, sudden, and unexpected attacks from the enemy. The enemy will want you to question God's Word and promises by drawing your attention to things that seemingly are not going right. But, lift up your shield of faith and protect yourself and *then get ready* to assault the strong man and completely overrun the stronghold while maintaining your stand.

"So then faith cometh by hearing, and hearing by the word of God" (Rom. 10:17). One of the assignments of the Holy Spirit in a believer's life is to put the believer in remembrance of the Word of God. Therefore, the more of the Word you have in you, the more the Holy Spirit will remind you of the Word in any particular situation. Conversely, if you do not study the Word, the Holy Spirit cannot remind you of the truth. Know that God has a word for every occasion.

Let us who live in the light keep sober, protected by the armor of faith and love, and wearing as our helmet, the happy hope of salvation. Cling tightly to your faith in Christ and always keep your conscience clear, doing what you know is right. Let us draw near to God with a true heart in full assurance of faith, because we have been sprinkled with Christ's blood to make us clean, because our bodies have been washed with pure water. Fight the good fight of faith (1 Thess. 5:8; 1 Tim. 1:19; Heb. 10:22; 1 Tim. 6:12).

Helmet of Salvation

The head is one of the most important parts of our bodies; and in God's design, it is encased in a protective skull. It is common to hear about heart transplants, about kidney transplants, and about other limbs of the body being transplanted. However, we never hear about a head transplant or brain transplant.

"For as he thinks in his heart, so is he" (Prov. 23:7). What controls your mind controls your life. If you think defeat, you walk in defeat. If you think sickness, you walk in sickness. The enemy will constantly bombard your mind with all manner of thoughts that will cripple your walk with God.

The helmet is designed to protect the head. It is designed to protect our minds and our whole attitude toward our Christian faith. If the enemy fails in damaging us in other ways, he will try to make us weary, discouraged, and disillusioned with evil thoughts and imaginations. *"For the weapons of our warfare are not carnal but mighty through God for the pulling down of strongholds, casting down imaginations and every high thing that exalts itself against the knowledge of God, and bringing every thought into captivity to the obedience of Christ. And having in a readiness to revenge all disobedience, when your obedience is fulfilled"* (2 Cor. 10:4).

To put on the helmet of salvation is to consistently read, study, and meditate on the Word of God. Meditation is to ponder, mutter, and reflect on the word. (It is not to make one's mind blank, as is taught by eastern religions. This eastern religious method opens your mind to demonic control.)

Weapons of Offense

Sword of the Spirit

"Take the sword of the Spirit, which is the word of God" (Eph 6:17b). A sword is a thrusting, striking, or cutting weapon with a long blade having one or more cutting edges. It is a weapon of offense which is used to attack an enemy. The enemy in this case is Satan and his hosts. When the enemy attacks us on any front, we use the other weapons for defense, to block the attack. When we are on the offensive, we attack him with the Word of God.

It is often said that the best form of defense is to attack. We cannot allow ourselves to be buffeted and attacked without response. We have to defend ourselves with the weapons of defense and *to attack* the enemy with the Word of God.

Always remember, that the arm of flesh will fail, but absolute reliance on God will lead to total victory. The Spirit of God—the Holy Spirit—the third person of the Trinity—will expressly carry out the promises in the Word, as long as we study and rightly appropriate Scripture to work on our behalf.

The best example for us to follow is found in the gospels where Jesus was tempted by the devil (Matt. 4:1-11; Mark 1:12-13; Luke

4:1-13). In all three accounts, Jesus quoted the Word and said, *"It is written."* Jesus overcame the devil with the Word of God. Friend, resist the devil with the Word of God, and he will flee!

Satan is a remarkably crafty, and an extremely wicked being, but Jesus has already overcome him. In that victory we still have the duty to study the Word and to enforce the will of God for our lives.

The Weapon of All Prayer

"Praying always with all prayer and supplication in the Spirit, and watching thereunto with all perseverance and supplication for all the saints" (Eph. 6:18).

Prayer has its own precepts. Among them:
- praying to God (Heb. 11:6)
- praying in the name of Jesus (John 14:6)
- praying in the Spirit (Eph. 6:18)
- praying according to the will of God (1 John 5:14)
- praying in faith (Eph. 3:20; James 1:6)
- praying earnestly (Luke 6:12)
- praying without hypocrisy (Matt. 6:5)

Ephesians 6:18 also teaches us how to pray, when to pray, the type of prayers to pray, and for whom to pray. *"Pray always"* with *"all prayer and supplication in the Spirit."* Furthermore, as you pray in the Spirit, the Holy Spirit helps you to pray over issues beyond your human understanding.

The weapon of *all prayer* means to pray with petitions and supplications. We must stand in the gap on behalf of others, to ask that the will of God be fulfilled in their lives. With this in mind, we take on our duty to be alert and keep praying for all the saints.

Chapter Seven

KEYS TO BINDING THE STRONG MAN

Jesus, full of the Holy Spirit, returned from the Jordan and was led by the Spirit into the desert, where for forty days He was tempted by the devil. He ate nothing during those days, and at the end of them He was hungry.

The devil said to him, 'If you are the Son of God, tell this stone to become bread.' Jesus answered, 'It is written: Man does not live by bread alone.'

The devil led Him up to a high place and showed Him in an instant all the kingdoms of the world. And he said to Him, 'I will give You all the authority and splendor for it has been given me, and I can give it to anyone I want to. So if You worship me, it will all be Yours.' Jesus answered, 'It is written: Worship the Lord your God and serve Him only.'

The devil led Him to Jerusalem and had Him stand on the highest point of the temple. 'If You are the Son of God,' he said, 'throw Yourself down from here. For it is written: He will command His angels concerning You to guard You carefully; they will lift You up in their hands, so that You will not strike Your foot against a stone.' Jesus answered, 'It is said: Do not put the Lord your God to the test.'

When the devil had finished all this tempting, he left Him until an opportune time. Jesus returned to Galilee in the power of the Spirit, and news about Him spread through the whole countryside.

Luke 4:1-14

From the Holy Scriptures we learn that our Lord Jesus Christ used five major keys of the kingdom to bind the strong man. He used the keys of:

- fasting
- prayer
- submission
- resistance
- the Word

1 - The key of Fasting

The Scripture says in Luke 4:2, *"Being forty days tempted of the devil. And in those days He did eat nothing: and when they were ended, He afterward hungered."* "He did eat nothing" means that He abstained from food which is carnal or fleshly—to be empowered spiritually. Fasting is a necessary tool and spiritual weapon every child of God must activate if the strong man is to be bound.

Friend, nothing substitutes for the key of fasting. It is necessary to understand that variant keys are meant for specified doors. You cannot use the key to the front door of the house to open the kitchen or the bedroom. Neither can you use the key to a Volkswagen to start a Mercedes. In the spiritual realm, specifically in the kingdom of God, various keys are meant for different functions. Different keys unlock the storehouses to different treasures of God.

The key of fasting unlocks the treasure of spiritual power. Our Lord Jesus Christ said, "Howbeit this kind goeth not out but by prayer and fasting" (Matt. 17:21). There are certain strong men that will not be bound except by fasting and prayer. Activate the spiritual weapons of fasting and prayer, and you will be amazed at the results in your life.

2 - The key of Prayer

The second key employed by our Lord Jesus Christ, in His supreme example as author and finisher of our faith, is the powerful weapon of prayer. Prayer is communication with God. Communication is a two-way flow of information. Most people assume that prayer is just talking to God, but that is absolutely not the case. Prayer is talking to God, and God talking back to you.

No other spiritual weapon or key substitutes the place of fervent prayer. Prayer must be fervent, intensive, persistent, and effective (James 5:16b). Jesus Christ, our High Priest, commands us to pray and not faint (Luke 18:1-8). The prayer that transcends the realm of the natural and penetrates the realm of the supernatural to bring into manifestation the purposes of God is agonizing, travailing prayer which is endless (Romans 8:26-27). Through prayer we fight the good fight of faith, and the strong man is bound.

Friend, employ the weapon of endless, ceaseless prayers with the Word of God and all satanic obstacles will give way for a full manifestation and demonstration of God's purposes for your life.

3 - The key of Submission

The third key that our Lord Jesus Christ used to bind the strong man is submission. Submission is willingly obeying instructions and given of oneself to a worthy cause—in this case, it is the Word of God.

In submission to God's Word, every attitude of rebellion, stubbornness, or disobedience is absolutely eliminated. According to the Scriptures, nobody can avenge any form of disobedience when obedience is incomplete. *"And we will be ready to punish every act of disobedience, once your obedience is complete"* (2 Cor. 10:6).

The Scripture also says, *"Submit yourself therefore to God. Resist the devil, and he will flee"* (James 4:7). Beloved, you can never give Satan commands for him to obey when you are not in obedience to God.

The story of Jesus and the centurion in the gospel according to Matthew gives us insight about what we are discussing. *"When Jesus had entered Capernaum, a centurion came to Him asking for help, 'Lord,' he said, 'my servant lies at home paralyzed and in terrible suffering.' Jesus said to him, 'I will go and heal him.' The centurion replied, 'Lord, I do not deserve to have You come under my roof. But just say the word, and my servant will be healed. For I myself am a man under authority, with soldiers under me. I tell this one, 'Go,' and he goes; and that one, 'Come,' and he comes. I say to my servant, 'Do this,' and he does it'"* (Matt. 8:5-10).

In verse nine, the centurion acknowledged that he was a man under authority. Being under authority is an attitude of submission. The absence of this vital virtue in the lives of the people of God has denied them the ability to bind the strong man.

There are three different kinds of authority: There are three kinds of authority—spiritual, civil, and domestic. Rebellion against any of these authorities is rebellion against God (Romans 13:1). Friend, remember that the devil, who was previously Lucifer, was the first among God's creatures to rebel. That is why we have sin in the world today. Because of this initial experience of rebellion, God does not tolerate it on any level.

If you are going to be able to bind the strong man, you should walk in absolute submission to the Word and the will of God at every stage and level of your life. *Submission is an indispensable weapon in binding the strong man.*

4 - The key of Resistance

The next key that our Lord and Savior Jesus Christ used was that of resistance. The word *resistance*, biblically speaking, means:
- to set against
- to withstand
- to stand firm against
- to rage in battle against
- to strive against
- to oppose

This is exactly what our Master and King did to the devil during the temptation in the wilderness. In spite of all the tricks and temptations of the enemy, Jesus Christ, our supreme example, withstood the enemy. The enemy was steadfastly resisted at every point of the battle. This attitude of our King and Supreme Conqueror did not occur only during the temptation in the wilderness, but was a lifestyle that was maintained all through the earthly ministry of the King of kings.

Friend, if the apostle and high priest of our profession had to resist the enemy every step of the way, you and I need to do the same even more so. The Scripture says, *"Be sober, be vigilant; because your adversary the devil, as a roaring lion, walketh about seeking whom he may devour: whom resist steadfast in the faith, knowing that the same afflictions are accomplished in your brethren that are in the world"* (1 Pet. 5:8-9).

The apostle Peter encourages believers to stand firm against the enemy. Throughout the Scriptures, anyone who had made a mark for God in his/her generation had to resist the enemy steadfastly.

Friend, you need to apply the key of resistance to bind the strong man. It is not just short-term, cozy, relaxed prayer that deals with the strong man! It is steadfast resistance coupled with all the other keys. You must refuse to be what the enemy wants you to be, and you must insist on God's prophetic agenda for your life to come to pass.

5 - The key of The Word of God

The Word of God is manifested in different dimensions. It is given to us as the written Word, the spoken Word, and the living Word. Jesus Christ, the Son of God, who walked on the shores of Galilee, is the living Word. The Scriptures say, *"In the beginning was the Word, and Word was with God, and the Word was God . . . And the Word was made flesh and dwelt among us, (and we beheld His glory, the glory as of the only begotten of the Father), full of grace and truth"* (John 1:1, 14). "The Word was made flesh and dwelt among us" talks of the incarnation of the Word of God as the living Word.

The spoken Word is the Word of God released as a two-edged sword from the mouth of the believer. The Bible says it is active and alive.

The written Word is the *logos,* that which has been recorded in the Scriptures.

All these manifestations of the Word of God are powerful and contain all the attributes of God. The Scriptures declare that, *"For in Him dwelleth all the fullness of the Godhead bodily. And ye are complete in Him which is the head of all principality and power"* (Col. 2:9-10). *"Jesus Christ is the same yesterday, today, and forever"* (Heb. 13:8).

The final key that Jesus Christ, the living Word, used to bind the strong man were the keys of the written Word and the spoken Word.

Friend, anywhere, anytime, and under any situation or circumstance that the strong man is confronted with the Word of God, he is totally overpowered. It is written that *"the light shineth in darkness, and the darkness cannot comprehend the power of the light"* (John 1:5). The strong man will always be bound when the Word of God is released against him. Too often many believers pray, shout, and make a lot of noise; but they do not speak the Word.

The centurion in the book of Matthew asked our Lord Jesus Christ not to worry Himself with coming over to the house, but to just speak the word, and his servant would be healed. Nothing is comparable with the spoken Word. Heaven and earth may pass, but the Word abides forever. *"Forever, O Lord, Thy Word is settled in heaven"* (Ps. 119:89).

The centurion had the revelation of authority. He knew that authority was to have one's words and commands obeyed. He also knew that the Lord Jesus Christ, the living Word, only had to release the spoken word, because He was (and still is) the One who has all authority. Sickness, or any other oppression, simply has to obey Him.

In Mark 5, the Bible speaks of a man bound with unclean spirits. This man was uncontrollable. On many occasions, he had been bound with chains; but he would break the chains and cut himself. His condition was hopeless. He was indwelt by a legion of demons. However, when Jesus Christ (the living Word) approached him and questioned the authority of the strong man that had bound this man, immediately, the strong man began to tremble, was driven out, and the man was clothed in his right senses (Mark 5:1-15).

Friend, enforce the Word of God, bind the strong man, and obtain notable miracles in every area of your life. "This book of the law shall not depart out of thy mouth; but thou shalt meditate therein day and night, that thou mayest observe to do according to all that is written therein: for thou shalt make thy way prosperous, and then thou shalt have good success" (Josh. 1:8).

Conclusion

Let me end with these reminders and exhortations for you. First, I want you to bear in mind that Satan, your adversary, is lurking around, ready for any occasion to attack you.

1. Renounce every un-confessed sin.
2. Renounce every case of information that the enemy has against you in his archives, in trees, rocks, water, in the heavenly realms. Negate it through the blood of Jesus.
3. Make this declaration:

I am redeemed from the hand of the devil by the blood of Jesus. I maintain my redemption rights, and I proclaim that through the blood of Jesus Christ, thrones, dominions, altars, principalities, powers, rulers of darkness, spiritual hosts of wickedness, and every satanic work have no authority over me.

I declare that the enemy is deprived of any access into my life and destiny. I maintain my God-given position in heavenly places, and the enemy is under my feet. Absolute victory is mine in Jesus' name.

"Be sober, be vigilant; because your adversary the devil walks about like a roaring lion, seeking whom he may devour. Resist him, steadfast in the faith." (1 Pet. 5:8). "Neither give place to the devil" (Eph. 4:27).

Secondly, it is important to remember that Satan has demons under his command, called the strong man, who desire to subject you to the devil's control. Bind the strong man aggressively, and claim your inheritance in Jesus' name.

Lastly, maintain your God-given freedom and liberty by standing firm in God. You can do this by:
- meditating on God's Word (Ps. 1:1-3);
- making prayer your habit (1 Thess. 5:17);
- finding a Bible-believing church;
- becoming active in the house of God. Spiritual idleness opens you to activities of demons and the strong man's gaining a hold over your life.

Prayer of Salvation

Lord, I confess that I am a sinner and I cannot save myself. I ask You, Lord, to forgive all my sins and wash me with the blood of Jesus Christ. I ask You, Lord Jesus, to come into my life and be my Lord and personal Savior. Fill me with Your Holy Spirit and write my name in the Book of Life. I pray this in the name of Jesus Christ, our Lord. Amen.

"Classics by the Archbishop"
Purchase the whole book series today!

Divine Timing

The Price of Greatness

The Supernatural Power of a Praying Man

The Incredible Power of a Praying Woman

Praying Through the Promises of God

Destined to Make an Impact

Binding The Strong Man

Enforcing Prophetic Decrees

For more information on
Archbishop Nicholas Duncan-Williams
and other powerful products,
please visit us online or contact
the office closest to you.

AFRICA
www.actionchapel.net
Tel: + (233) 21.701.1851 (GHANA)

EUROPE
www.actionchapel.co.uk
Tel: + (44) 0208.952.0626 (UK)

NORTH AMERICA
www.prayersummitint.com
or call + (001) 202.587.2720. (USA)

Action Worship Center, Maryland
www.actionworshipcenter.net
+ (001) 301.498.7501

Action Chapel VA, Virginia
www.actionchapelva.org
+ (001) 703.224.8107

CPSIA information can be obtained
at www.ICGtesting.com
Printed in the USA
LVHW031144200319
611264LV00001B/169/P